THE BIBLE SPEAKS ABOUT FAITH

Daily Readings
from the Authorised, or King James, Version
and the New English Bible

THE BIBLE SPEAKS ABOUT FAITH

Daily Readings
from the Authorised, or King James, Version
and the New English Bible

Chosen and Arranged by
CECIL NORTHCOTT

ASSOCIATION PRESS, NEW YORK

These daily readings from the Bible are chosen from the Authorised, or King James, Version of the Bible, and the New English Bible, as a testimony to the Bible's continuous power to build a believer's faith and to give him guidance for daily living.

Placed side by side the passages show how old and new versions of the Bible taken together throw fresh light on Christian truth.

Blessed are the poor in spirit: for theirs is the kingdom of heaven.

Blessed are they that mourn: for they shall be comforted.

Blessed are the meek: for they shall inherit the earth.

Blessed are they which do hunger and thirst after righteousness: for they shall be filled.

Blessed are the merciful: for they shall obtain mercy.

Blessed are the pure in heart: for they shall see God.

Blessed are the peacemakers: for they shall be called the children of God.

Blessed are they which are persecuted for righteousness' sake: for theirs is the kingdom of heaven.

Matthew 5: 3–10

"How blest are those who know that they are poor;
   the kingdom of Heaven is theirs.
How blest are the sorrowful;
   they shall find consolation.
How blest are those of a gentle spirit;
   they shall have the earth for their possession.
How blest are those who hunger and thirst to see right prevail;
   they shall be satisfied.
How blest are those who show mercy;
   mercy shall be shown to them.
How blest are those whose hearts are pure;
   they shall see God.
How blest are the peacemakers;
   God shall call them his sons.
How blest are those who have suffered persecution for the
   cause of right;
   the kingdom of Heaven is theirs."

Matthew 5: 3–10

1ST DAY

But seek ye first the kingdom of God, and his righteousness; and all these things shall be added unto you.

Take therefore no thought for the morrow: for the morrow shall take thought for the things of itself. Sufficient unto the day is the evil thereof.

Matthew 6: 33–34

MY YOKE IS EASY

Come unto me, all ye that labour and are heavy laden, and I will give you rest.

Take my yoke upon you, and learn of me; for I am meek and lowly in heart: and ye shall find rest unto your souls.

For my yoke is easy, and my burden is light.

Matthew 11: 28–30

"Set your mind on God's kingdom and his justice before everything else, and all the rest will come to you as well. So do not be anxious about tomorrow; tomorrow will look after itself. Each day has troubles enough of its own."

Matthew 6: 33–34

MY YOKE IS GOOD

"Come to me, all whose work is hard, whose load is heavy; and I will give you relief. Bend your necks to my yoke, and learn from me, for I am gentle and humble-hearted; and your souls will find relief. For my yoke is good to bear, my load is light."

Matthew 11: 28–30

And Peter answered him and said, Lord, if it be thou, bid me come unto thee on the water.

And he said, Come. And when Peter was come down out of the ship, he walked on the water, to go to Jesus.

But when he saw the wind boisterous, he was afraid; and beginning to sink, he cried, saying, Lord, save me.

And immediately Jesus stretched forth his hand, and caught him, and said unto him, O thou of little faith, wherefore didst thou doubt?

And when they were come into the ship, the wind ceased.

Then they that were in the ship came and worshipped him, saying, Of a truth thou art the Son of God.

Matthew 14: 28–33

SHALL FIND LIFE

Then said Jesus unto his disciples, If any man will come after me, let him deny himself, and take up his cross, and follow me.

For whosoever will save his life shall lose it: and whosoever will lose his life for my sake shall find it.

Matthew 16: 24–25

3RD DAY

Peter called to him: "Lord, if it is you, tell me to come to you over the water." "Come," said Jesus. Peter stepped down from the boat, and walked over the water towards Jesus. But when he saw the strength of the gale he was seized with fear; and beginning to sink, he cried, "Save me, Lord." Jesus at once reached out and caught hold of him, and said, "Why did you hesitate? How little faith you have!" They then climbed into the boat; and the wind dropped. And the men in the boat fell at his feet, exclaiming, "Truly you are the Son of God."

Matthew 14: 28–33

FIND HIS TRUE SELF

Jesus then said to his disciples, "If anyone wishes to be a follower of mine, he must leave self behind; he must take up his cross and come with me. Whoever cares for his own safety is lost; but if a man will let himself be lost for my sake, he will find his true self."

Matthew 16: 24–25

3RD DAY

At the same time came the disciples unto Jesus, saying, Who is the greatest in the kingdom of heaven?

And Jesus called a little child unto him, and set him in the midst of them,

And said, Verily I say unto you, Except ye be converted, and become as little children, ye shall not enter into the kingdom of heaven.

Whosoever therefore shall humble himself as this little child, the same is greatest in the kingdom of heaven.

Matthew 18: 1–4

IF THOU WILT BE PERFECT

And, behold, one came and said unto him, Good Master, what good thing shall I do, that I may have eternal life? . . .

The young man saith unto him, What lack I yet?

Jesus said unto him, If thou wilt be perfect, go and sell that thou hast, and give to the poor, and thou shalt have treasure in heaven: and come and follow me.

But when the young man heard that saying, he went away sorrowful: for he had great possessions.

Matthew 19: 16, 20–22

4TH DAY

At that time the disciples came to Jesus and asked, "Who is the greatest in the kingdom of Heaven?" He called a child, set him in front of them, and said, "I tell you this: unless you turn round and become like children, you will never enter the kingdom of Heaven. Let a man humble himself till he is like this child, and he will be the greatest in the kingdom of Heaven."

Matthew 18: 1–4

GO THE WHOLE WAY

And now a man came up and asked him, "Master, what good must I do to gain eternal life?" . . .

The young man answered, "Where do I still fall short?" Jesus said to him, "If you wish to go the whole way, go, sell your possessions, and give to the poor, and then you will have riches in heaven; and come, follow me." When the young man heard this, he went away with a heavy heart; for he was a man of great wealth.

Matthew 19: 16, 20–22

4TH DAY

And he asked his father, How long is it ago since this came unto him? And he said, Of a child.

And ofttimes it hath cast him into the fire, and into the waters, to destroy him: but if thou canst do any thing, have compassion on us, and help us.

Jesus said unto him, If thou canst believe, all things are possible to him that believeth.

And straightway the father of the child cried out, and said with tears, Lord, I believe; help thou mine unbelief.

Mark 9: 21–24

RISE; HE CALLETH THEE

And they call the blind man, saying unto him, Be of good comfort, rise; he calleth thee.

And he, casting away his garment, rose, and came to Jesus.

And Jesus answered and said unto him, What wilt thou that I should do unto thee? The blind man said unto him, Lord, that I might receive my sight.

And Jesus said unto him, Go thy way; thy faith hath made thee whole. And immediately he received his sight, and followed Jesus in the way.

Mark 10: 49–52

Jesus asked his father, "How long has he been like this?" "From childhood," he replied; "often it has tried to make an end of him by throwing him into the fire or into water. But if it is at all possible for you, take pity upon us and help us." "If it is possible!" said Jesus. "Everything is possible to one who has faith." "I have faith," cried the boy's father; "help me where faith falls short."

Mark 9: 21–24

STAND UP; HE IS CALLING

So they called the blind man and said, "Take heart; stand up; he is calling you." At that he threw off his cloak, sprang up, and came to Jesus. Jesus said to him, "What do you want me to do for you?" "Master," the blind man answered, "I want my sight back." Jesus said to him, "Go; your faith has cured you." And at once he recovered his sight and followed him on the road.

Mark 10: 49–52

5TH DAY

And Jesus answering saith unto them, Have faith in God. For verily I say unto you, That whosoever shall say unto this mountain, Be thou removed, and be thou cast into the sea; and shall not doubt in his heart, but shall believe that those things which he saith shall come to pass; he shall have whatsoever he saith.

Mark 11: 22–23

THY SINS ARE FORGIVEN

And, behold, men brought in a bed a man which was taken with a palsy: and they sought means to bring him in, and to lay him before him.

And when they could not find by what way they might bring him in because of the multitude, they went upon the housetop, and let him down through the tiling with his couch into the midst before Jesus.

And when he saw their faith, he said unto him, Man, thy sins are forgiven thee.

Luke 5: 18–20

6TH DAY

Jesus answered them, "Have faith in God. I tell you this: if anyone says to this mountain, 'Be lifted from your place and hurled into the sea', and has no inward doubts, but believes that what he says is happening, it will be done for him. I tell you, then, whatever you ask for in prayer, believe that you have received it and it will be yours."

Mark 11: 22–24

MAN, YOU ARE FORGIVEN

Some men appeared carrying a paralysed man on a bed. They tried to bring him in and set him down in front of Jesus, but finding no way to do so because of the crowd, they went up on to the roof and let him down through the tiling, bed and all, into the middle of the company in front of Jesus.

When Jesus saw their faith, he said, "Man, your sins are forgiven you."

Luke 5: 18–20

Judge not, and ye shall not be judged: condemn not, and ye shall not be condemned: forgive, and ye shall be forgiven:

Give, and it shall be given unto you; good measure, pressed down, and shaken together, and running over, shall men give into your bosom. For with the same measure that ye mete withal it shall be measured to you again.

Luke 6: 37–38

ABUNDANCE OF THE HEART

For a good tree bringeth not forth corrupt fruit; neither doth a corrupt tree bring forth good fruit.

For every tree is known by his own fruit. For of thorns men do not gather figs, nor of a bramble bush gather they grapes.

A good man out of the good treasure of his heart bringeth forth that which is good; and an evil man out of the evil treasure of his heart bringeth forth that which is evil: for of the abundance of the heart his mouth speaketh.

Luke 6: 43–45

7TH DAY

"Pass no judgement, and you will not be judged; do not condemn, and you will not be condemned; acquit, and you will be acquitted; give, and gifts will be given you. Good measure, pressed down, shaken together, and running over, will be poured into your lap; for whatever measure you deal out to others will be dealt to you in return."

Luke 6: 37-38

THE OVERFLOWING HEART

"There is no such thing as a good tree producing worthless fruit, nor yet a worthless tree producing good fruit. For each tree is known by its own fruit: you do not gather figs from thistles, and you do not pick grapes from brambles. A good man produces good from the store of good within himself; and an evil man from evil within produces evil. For the words that the mouth utters come from the overflowing of the heart."

Luke 6: 43–45

7TH DAY

And he spake a parable unto them, saying, The ground of a certain rich man brought forth plentifully:

And he thought within himself, saying, What shall I do, because I have no room where to bestow my fruits?

And he said, This will I do: I will pull down my barns, and build greater; and there will I bestow all my fruits and my goods.

And I will say to my soul, Soul, thou hast much goods laid up for many years; take thine ease, eat, drink, and be merry.

But God said unto him, Thou fool, this night thy soul shall be required of thee: then whose shall those things be, which thou hast provided?

So is he that layeth up treasure for himself, and is not rich toward God.

Luke 12: 16–21

THE GOOD PART

But Martha was cumbered about much serving, and came to him, and said, Lord, dost thou not care that my sister hath left me to serve alone? bid her therefore that she help me.

And Jesus answered and said unto her, Martha, Martha, thou art careful and troubled about many things:

But one thing is needful: and Mary hath chosen that good part, which shall not be taken away from her.

Luke 10: 40–42

8TH DAY

And he told them this parable: "There was a rich man whose land yielded heavy crops. He debated with himself: 'What am I to do? I have not the space to store my produce. This is what I will do,' said he: 'I will pull down my storehouses and build them bigger. I will collect in them all my corn and other goods, and then say to myself, "Man, you have plenty of good things laid by, enough for many years: take life easy, eat, drink, and enjoy yourself." ' But God said to him, 'You fool, this very night you must surrender your life; you have made your money—who will get it now?' That is how it is with the man who amasses wealth for himself and remains a pauper in the sight of God."

Luke 12: 16–21

THE CHOSEN PART

Now Martha was distracted by her many tasks, so she came to him and said: "Lord, do you not care that my sister has left me to get on with the work by myself? Tell her to come and lend a hand." But the Lord answered: "Martha, Martha, you are fretting and fussing about so many things; but one thing is necessary. The part that Mary has chosen is best; and it shall not be taken away from her."

Luke 10: 40–42

8TH DAY

No man, when he hath lighted a candle, putteth it in a secret place, neither under a bushel, but on a candlestick, that they which come in may see the light.

The light of the body is the eye: therefore when thine eye is single, thy whole body also is full of light; but when thine eye is evil, thy body also is full of darkness.

Take heed therefore that the light which is in thee be not darkness.

If thy whole body therefore be full of light, having no part dark, the whole shall be full of light, as when the bright shining of a candle doth give thee light.

Luke 11: 33–36

BAGS WHICH WAX NOT OLD

Fear not, little flock; for it is your Father's good pleasure to give you the kingdom.

Sell that ye have, and give alms; provide yourselves bags which wax not old, a treasure in the heavens that faileth not, where no thief approacheth, neither moth corrupteth.

For where your treasure is, there will your heart be also.

Luke 12: 32–34

9TH DAY

"No one lights a lamp and puts it in a cellar, but rather on the lamp-stand so that those who enter may see the light. The lamp of your body is the eye. When your eyes are sound, you have light for your whole body; but when the eyes are bad, you are in darkness. See to it then that the light you have is not darkness. If you have light for your whole body with no trace of darkness, it will all be as bright as when a lamp flashes its rays upon you."

Luke 11: 33–36

PURSES THAT DON'T WEAR OUT

"Have no fear, little flock; for your Father has chosen to give you the Kingdom. Sell your possessions and give in charity. Provide for yourselves purses that do not wear out, and never-failing wealth in heaven, where no thief can get near it, no moth destroy it. For where your wealth is, there will your heart be also."

Luke 12: 32–34

9TH DAY

Consider the lilies how they grow: they toil not, they spin not; and yet I say unto you, that Solomon in all his glory was not arrayed like one of these.

If then God so clothe the grass, which is to day in the field, and to morrow is cast into the oven; how much more will he clothe you, O ye of little faith?

And seek not ye what ye shall eat, or what ye shall drink, neither be ye of doubtful mind.

For all these things do the nations of the world seek after: and your Father knoweth that ye have need of these things.

But rather seek ye the kingdom of God; and all these things shall be added unto you.

Luke 12: 27–31

TAKE HEED

And take heed to yourselves, lest at any time your hearts be overcharged with surfeiting, and drunkenness, and cares of this life, and so that day come upon you unawares.

For as a snare shall it come on all them that dwell on the face of the whole earth.

Watch ye therefore, and pray always, that ye may be accounted worthy to escape all these things that shall come to pass, and to stand before the Son of man.

Luke 21: 34–36

10TH DAY

"Think of the lilies: they neither spin nor weave; yet I tell you, even Solomon in all his splendour was not attired like one of these. But if that is how God clothes the grass, which is growing in the field today, and tomorrow is thrown on the stove, how much more will he clothe you! How little faith you have! And so you are not to set your mind on food and drink; you are not to worry. For all these are things for the heathen to run after; but you have a Father who knows that you need them. No, set your mind upon his kingdom, and all the rest will come to you as well."

Luke 12: 27–31

KEEP A WATCH

"Keep a watch on yourselves; do not let your minds be dulled by dissipation and drunkenness and worldly cares so that the great Day closes upon you suddenly like a trap; for that day will come on all men, wherever they are, the whole world over. Be on the alert, praying at all times for strength to pass safely through all these imminent troubles and to stand in the presence of the Son of Man."

Luke 21: 34–36

10TH DAY

Verily, verily, I say unto you, He that heareth my word, and believeth on him that sent me, hath everlasting life, and shall not come into condemnation; but is passed from death unto life.

Verily, verily, I say unto you, The hour is coming, and now is, when the dead shall hear the voice of the Son of God: and they that hear shall live.

For as the Father hath life in himself; so hath he given to the Son to have life in himself.

John 5: 24–26

NEITHER BE AFRAID

Peace I leave with you, my peace I give unto you: not as the world giveth, give I unto you. Let not your heart be troubled, neither let it be afraid.

Ye have heard how I said unto you, I go away, and come again unto you. If ye loved me, ye would rejoice, because I said, I go unto the Father: for my Father is greater than I.

And now I have told you before it come to pass, that, when it is come to pass, ye might believe.

John 14: 27–29

11TH DAY

"In very truth, anyone who gives heed to what I say and puts his trust in him who sent me has hold of eternal life, and does not come up for judgement, but has already passed from death to life. In truth, in very truth I tell you, a time is coming, indeed it is already here, when the dead shall hear the voice of the Son of God, and all who hear shall come to life. For as the Father has life-giving power in himself, so has the Son, by the Father's gift."

John 5: 24–26

BANISH YOUR FEARS

"Peace is my parting gift to you, my own peace, such as the world cannot give. Set your troubled hearts at rest, and banish your fears. You heard me say, 'I am going away, and coming back to you.' If you loved me you would have been glad to hear that I was going to the Father; for the Father is greater than I. I have told you now, beforehand, so that when it happens you may have faith."

John 14: 27–29

11TH DAY

Whom God hath set forth to be a propitiation through faith in his blood, to declare his righteousness for the remission of sins that are past, through the forbearance of God;

To declare, I say, at this time his righteousness: that he might be just, and the justifier of him which believeth in Jesus.

Romans 3: 25–26

ALL THE SEED

Therefore it is of faith, that it might be by grace; to the end the promise might be sure to all the seed; not to that only which is of the law, but to that also which is of the faith of Abraham; who is the father of us all.

Romans 4: 16

For God designed him to be the means of expiating sin by his sacrificial death, effective through faith. God meant by this to demonstrate his justice, because in his forbearance he had overlooked the sins of the past—to demonstrate his justice now in the present, showing that he is both himself just and justifies any man who puts his faith in Jesus.

Romans 3: 25–26

VALID FOR ALL

The promise was made on the ground of faith, in order that it might be a matter of sheer grace, and that it might be valid for all Abraham's posterity, not only for those who hold by the law, but for those also who have the faith of Abraham.

Romans 4: 16

Therefore being justified by faith, we have peace with God through our Lord Jesus Christ:

By whom also we have access by faith into this grace wherein we stand, and rejoice in hope of the glory of God.

Romans 5: 1–2

FREE FROM SIN

But now being made free from sin, and become servants to God, ye have your fruit unto holiness, and the end everlasting life.

For the wages of sin is death; but the gift of God is eternal life through Jesus Christ our Lord.

Romans 6: 22–23

ENTER THE SPHERE OF GRACE

Therefore, now that we have been justified through faith, let us continue at peace with God through our Lord Jesus Christ, through whom we have been allowed to enter the sphere of God's grace, where we now stand. Let us exult in the hope of the divine splendour that is to be ours.

Romans 5: 1–2

FREED FROM THE COMMANDS OF SIN

But now, freed from the commands of sin, and bound to the service of God, your gains are such as make for holiness, and the end is eternal life. For sin pays a wage, and the wage is death, but God gives freely, and his gift is eternal life, in union with Christ Jesus our Lord.

Romans 6: 22–23

13TH DAY

For I am persuaded, that neither death, nor life, nor angels, nor principalities, nor powers, nor things present, nor things to come,

Nor height, nor depth, nor any other creature, shall be able to separate us from the love of God, which is in Christ Jesus our Lord.

Romans 8: 38–39

THOU SHALT BE SAVED

If thou shalt confess with thy mouth the Lord Jesus, and shalt believe in thine heart that God hath raised him from the dead, thou shalt be saved.

For with the heart man believeth unto righteousness; and with the mouth confession is made unto salvation.

Romans 10: 9–10

For I am convinced that there is nothing in death or life, in the realm of spirits or superhuman powers, in the world as it is or the world as it shall be, in the forces of the universe, in heights or depths—nothing in all creation that can separate us from the love of God in Christ Jesus our Lord.

Romans 8: 38–39

YOU WILL FIND SALVATION

If on your lips is the confession, "Jesus is Lord", and in your heart the faith that God raised him from the dead, then you will find salvation. For the faith that leads to righteousness is in the heart, and the confession that leads to salvation is upon the lips.

Romans 10: 9–10

14TH DAY
C

O the depth of the riches both of the wisdom and knowledge of God! how unsearchable are his judgments, and his ways past finding out!

For who hath known the mind of the Lord? or who hath been his counseller?

Or who hath first given to him, and it shall be recompensed unto him again?

For of him, and through him, and to him, are all things: to whom be glory for ever. Amen.

Romans 11: 33–36

WITH THE TEMPTATION

Wherefore let him that thinketh he standeth take heed lest he fall.

There hath no temptation taken you but such as is common to man: but God is faithful, who will not suffer you to be tempted above that ye are able; but will with the temptation also make a way to escape, that ye may be able to bear it.

1 *Corinthians* 10: 12, 13

15TH DAY

O depth of wealth, wisdom, and knowledge in God! How unsearchable his judgements, how untraceable his ways! Who knows the mind of the Lord? Who has been his counsellor? Who has ever made a gift to him, to receive a gift in return? Source, Guide, and Goal of all that is—to him be glory for ever! Amen.

Romans 11: 33–36

WHEN THE TEST COMES

If you feel sure that you are standing firm, beware! You may fall. So far you have faced no trial beyond what man can bear. God keeps faith, and he will not allow you to be tested above your powers, but when the test comes he will at the same time provide a way out, by enabling you to sustain it.

1 *Corinthians* 10: 12, 13

15TH DAY

Though I speak with the tongues of men and of angels, and have not charity, I am become as sounding brass, or a tinkling cymbal.

And though I have the gift of prophecy, and understand all mysteries, and all knowledge; and though I have all faith, so that I could remove mountains, and have not charity, I am nothing.

And though I bestow all my goods to feed the poor, and though I give my body to be burned, and have not charity, it profiteth me nothing.

1 Corinthians 13: 1–3

NOT DESTROYED

We are troubled on every side, yet not distressed; we are perplexed, but not in despair;

Persecuted, but not forsaken; cast down, but not destroyed;

Always bearing about in the body the dying of the Lord Jesus, that the life also of Jesus might be made manifest in our body.

2 Corinthians 4: 8–10

16TH DAY

IF I HAVE NO LOVE

I may speak in tongues of men or of angels, but if I am without love, I am a sounding gong or a clanging cymbal. I may have the gift of prophecy, and know every hidden truth; I may have faith strong enough to move mountains; but if I have no love, I am nothing. I may dole out all I possess, or even give my body to be burnt, but if I have no love, I am none the better.

1 *Corinthians* 13: 1-3

WE ARE NOT LEFT TO DIE

Hard-pressed on every side, we are never hemmed in; bewildered, we are never at our wits' end; hunted, we are never abandoned to our fate; struck down, we are not left to die. Wherever we go we carry death with us in our body, the death that Jesus died, that in this body also life may reveal itself, the life that Jesus lives.

2 *Corinthians* 4: 8-10

16TH DAY

Examine yourselves, whether ye be in the faith; prove your own selves. Know ye not your own selves, how that Jesus Christ is in you, except ye be reprobates?

But I trust that ye shall know that we are not reprobates.

Now I pray to God that ye do no evil; not that we should appear approved, but that ye should do that which is honest, though we be as reprobates.

2 Corinthians 13 : 5–7

SUFFICIENCY OF GOD

Not that we are sufficient of ourselves to think any thing as of ourselves; but our sufficiency is of God;

Who also hath made us able ministers of the new testament; not of the letter, but of the spirit: for the letter killeth, but the spirit giveth life.

2 Corinthians 3 : 5–6

Examine yourselves: are you living the life of faith? Put yourselves to the test. Surely you recognize that Jesus Christ is among you?—unless of course you prove unequal to the test. I hope you will come to see that we are not unequal to it. Our prayer to God is that we may not have to hurt you; we are not concerned to be vindicated ourselves; we want you to do what is right, even if we should seem to be discredited.

2 Corinthians 13 : 5–7

QUALIFICATION FROM GOD

There is no question of our being qualified in ourselves: we cannot claim anything as our own. Such qualification as we have comes from God; it is he who has qualified us to dispense his new covenant—a covenant expressed not in a written document, but in a spiritual bond; for the written law condemns to death, but the Spirit gives life.

2 Corinthians 3 : 5–6

17TH DAY

But this I say, He which soweth sparingly shall reap also sparingly; and he which soweth bountifully shall reap also bountifully.

Every man according as he purposeth in his heart, so let him give; not grudgingly, or of necessity: for God loveth a cheerful giver.

And God is able to make all grace abound toward you; that ye, always having all sufficiency in all things, may abound to every good work.

2 Corinthians 9: 6–8

I LIVE; YET NOT I

I am crucified with Christ: nevertheless I live; yet not I, but Christ liveth in me: and the life which I now live in the flesh I live by the faith of the Son of God, who loved me, and gave himself for me.

I do not frustrate the grace of God: for if righteousness come by the law, then Christ is dead in vain.

Galatians 2: 20–21

Remember: sparse sowing, sparse reaping; sow bountifully, and you will reap bountifully. Each person should give as he has decided for himself; there should be no reluctance, no sense of compulsion; God loves a cheerful giver. And it is in God's power to provide you richly with every good gift; thus you will have ample means in yourselves to meet each and every situation, with enough and to spare for every good cause.

2 Corinthians 9: 6–8

THE LIFE IS NOT MY LIFE

I have been crucified with Christ: the life I now live is not my life, but the life which Christ lives in me; and my present bodily life is lived by faith in the Son of God, who loved me and sacrificed himself for me. I will not nullify the grace of God; if righteousness comes by law, then Christ died for nothing.

Galatians 2: 20–21

18TH DAY

But before faith came, we were kept under the law, shut up unto the faith which should afterwards be revealed.

Wherefore the law was our schoolmaster to bring us unto Christ, that we might be justified by faith.

But after that faith is come, we are no longer under a schoolmaster.

Galatians 3: 23–25

WALK AS CHILDREN OF LIGHT

Be not ye therefore partakers with them.

For ye were sometimes darkness, but now are ye light in the Lord: walk as children of light:

(For the fruit of the Spirit is in all goodness and righteousness and truth;)

Proving what is acceptable unto the Lord.

And have no fellowship with the unfruitful works of darkness, but rather reprove them.

For it is a shame even to speak of those things which are done of them in secret.

Ephesians 5: 7–12

19TH DAY

Before this faith came, we were close prisoners in the custody of law, pending the revelation of faith. Thus the law was a kind of tutor in charge of us until Christ should come, when we should be justified through faith; and now that faith has come, the tutor's charge is at an end.

Galatians 3: 23–25

LIVE LIKE MEN IN DAYLIGHT

Have no part or lot with them. For though you were once all darkness, now as Christians you are light. Live like men who are at home in daylight, for where light is, there all goodness springs up, all justice and truth. Make sure what would have the Lord's approval; take no part in the barren deeds of darkness, but show them up for what they are. The things they do in secret it would be shameful even to mention.

Ephesians 5: 7–12

S tand therefore, having your loins girt about with truth, and having on the breastplate of righteousness;

And your feet shod with the preparation of the gospel of peace;

Above all, taking the shield of faith, wherewith ye shall be able to quench all the fiery darts of the wicked.

And take the helmet of salvation, and the sword of the Spirit, which is the word of God.

Ephesians 6: 14–17

THE BUILDING FITLY FRAMED

A nd are built upon the foundation of the apostles and prophets, Jesus Christ himself being the chief corner stone;

In whom all the building fitly framed together groweth unto an holy temple in the Lord:

In whom ye also are builded together for an habitation of God through the Spirit.

Ephesians 2: 20–22

S tand firm, I say. Buckle on the belt of truth; for coat of
mail put on integrity; let the shoes on your feet be the
gospel of peace, to give you firm footing; and, with all these,
take up the great shield of faith, with which you will be able
to quench all the flaming arrows of the evil one. Take salvation for helmet; for sword, take that which the Spirit gives
you—the words that come from God.

Ephesians 6: 14–17

THE BUILDING IS BONDED

Y ou are built upon the foundation laid by the apostles and
prophets, and Christ Jesus himself is the foundation-
stone. In him the whole building is bonded together and
grows into a holy temple in the Lord. In him you too are
being built with all the rest into a spiritual dwelling for God.

Ephesians 2: 20–22

20TH DAY

ROOTED AND GROUNDED KJV

That Christ may dwell in your hearts by faith; that ye, being rooted and grounded in love,

May be able to comprehend with all saints what is the breadth, and length, and depth, and height;

And to know the love of Christ, which passeth knowledge, that ye might be filled with all the fulness of God.

Ephesians 3 : 17-19

THE THINGS WHICH ARE BEFORE

Brethren, I count not myself to have apprehended: but this one thing I do, forgetting those things which are behind, and reaching forth unto those things which are before,

I press toward the mark for the prize of the high calling of God in Christ Jesus.

Philippians 3 : 13-14

With deep roots and firm foundations, may you be strong to grasp, with all God's people, what is the breadth and length and height and depth of the love of Christ, and to know it, though it is beyond knowledge. So may you attain to fullness of being, the fullness of God himself.

Ephesians 3: 17–19

THAT WHICH LIES AHEAD

All I can say is this: forgetting what is behind me, and reaching out for that which lies ahead, I press towards the goal to win the prize which is God's call to the life above, in Christ Jesus.

Philippians 3: 13–14

21ST DAY

BE LIKE-MINDED KJV

If there be therefore any consolation in Christ, if any comfort of love, if any fellowship of the Spirit, if any bowels and mercies,

Fulfil ye my joy, that ye be like-minded, having the same love, being of one accord, of one mind.

Philippians 2: 1–2

GOD'S WORD—QUICK AND POWERFUL

For the word of God is quick, and powerful, and sharper than any two-edged sword, piercing even to the dividing asunder of soul and spirit, and of the joints and marrow, and is a discerner of the thoughts and intents of the heart.

Neither is there any creature that is not manifest in his sight: but all things are naked and opened unto the eyes of him with whom we have to do.

Hebrews 4: 12–13

22ND DAY

I f then our common life in Christ yields anything to stir the heart, any loving consolation, any sharing of the Spirit, any warmth of affection or compassion, fill up my cup of happiness by thinking and feeling alike, with the same love for one another, the same turn of mind, and a common care for unity.

Philippians 2: 1–2

GOD'S WORD—ALIVE AND ACTIVE

F or the word of God is alive and active. It cuts more keenly than any two-edged sword, piercing as far as the place where life and spirit, joints and marrow, divide. It sifts the purposes and thoughts of the heart. There is nothing in creation that can hide from him; everything lies naked and exposed to the eyes of the One with whom we have to reckon.

Hebrews 4: 12–13

22ND DAY
D

But Christ being come an high priest of good things to come, by a greater and more perfect tabernacle, not made with hands, that is to say, not of this building;

Neither by the blood of goats and calves, but by his own blood he entered in once into the holy place, having obtained eternal redemption for us.

Hebrews 9: 11–12

NOT CARRIED ABOUT

Jesus Christ the same yesterday, and to day, and for ever.

Be not carried about with divers and strange doctrines. For it is a good thing that the heart be established with grace; not with meats, which have not profited them that have been occupied therein.

Hebrews 13: 8–9

But now Christ has come, high priest of good things already in being. The tent of his priesthood is a greater and more perfect one, not made by men's hands, that is, not belonging to this created world; the blood of his sacrifice is his own blood, not the blood of goats and calves; and thus he has entered the sanctuary 'once and for all and secured an eternal deliverance.

Hebrews 9: 11-12

NOT SWEPT OFF YOUR COURSE

Jesus Christ is the same yesterday, today, and for ever. So do not be swept off your course by all sorts of outlandish teachings; it is good that our souls should gain their strength from the grace of God, and not from scruples about what we eat, which have never done any good to those who were governed by them.

Hebrews 13: 8-9

Wherefore seeing we also are compassed about with so great a cloud of witnesses, let us lay aside every weight, and the sin which doth so easily beset us, and let us run with patience the race that is set before us,

Looking unto Jesus the author and finisher of our faith; who for the joy that was set before him endured the cross, despising the shame, and is set down at the right hand of the throne of God.

Hebrews 12: 1–2

SUBSTANCE OF THINGS HOPED FOR

Now faith is the substance of things hoped for, the evidence of things not seen.

For by it the elders obtained a good report.

Through faith we understand that the worlds were framed by the word of God, so that things which are seen were not made of things which do appear.

Hebrews 11: 1–3

And what of ourselves? With all these witnesses to faith around us like a cloud, we must throw off every encumbrance, every sin to which we cling, and run with resolution the race for which we are entered, our eyes fixed on Jesus, on whom faith depends from start to finish: Jesus who, for the sake of the joy that lay ahead of him, endured the cross, making light of its disgrace, and has taken his seat at the right hand of the throne of God.

Hebrews 12: 1–2

SUBSTANCE TO OUR HOPES

And what is faith? Faith gives substance to our hopes, and makes us certain of realities we do not see.

It is for their faith that the men of old stand on record.

By faith we perceive that the universe was fashioned by the word of God, so that the visible came forth from the invisible.

Hebrews 11: 1–3

But thou, O man of God, flee these things; and follow after righteousness, godliness, faith, love, patience, meekness.

Fight the good fight of faith, lay hold on eternal life, whereunto thou art also called, and hast professed a good profession before many witnesses.

I give thee charge in the sight of God, who quickeneth all things, and before Christ Jesus, who before Pontius Pilate witnessed a good confession.

1 Timothy 6: 11–13

COMMITTED UNTO HIM

Whereunto I am appointed a preacher, and an apostle, and a teacher of the Gentiles.

For the which cause I also suffer these things: nevertheless I am not ashamed: for I know whom I have believed, and am persuaded that he is able to keep that which I have committed unto him against that day.

2 Timothy 1: 11–12

25TH DAY

But you, man of God, must shun all this, and pursue justice, piety, fidelity, love, fortitude, and gentleness. Run the great race of faith and take hold of eternal life. For to this you were called; and you confessed your faith nobly before many witnesses. Now in the presence of God, who gives life to all things, and of Jesus Christ, who himself made the same noble confession and gave his testimony to it before Pontius Pilate.

1 *Timothy* 6: 11–13

IN WHOM I HAVE TRUSTED

Of this Gospel I, by his appointment, am herald, apostle, and teacher. That is the reason for my present plight; but I am not ashamed of it, because I know who it is in whom I have trusted, and am confident of his power to keep safe what he has put into my charge, until the great Day.

2 *Timothy* 1: 11–12

25TH DAY

Ⓑut continue thou in the things which thou hast learned and hast been assured of, knowing of whom thou hast learned them;

And that from a child thou hast known the holy scriptures, which are able to make thee wise unto salvation through faith which is in Christ Jesus.

2 Timothy 3 : 14–15

A MAN THAT WARRETH

Ⓣhou therefore endure hardness, as a good soldier of Jesus Christ.

No man that warreth entangleth himself with the affairs of this life; that he may please him who hath chosen him to be a soldier.

And if a man also strive for masteries, yet is he not crowned, except he strive lawfully.

The husbandman that laboureth must be first partaker of the fruits.

Consider what I say; and the Lord give thee understanding in all things.

2 Timothy 2 : 3–7

26TH DAY

B ut for your part, stand by the truths you have learned
and are assured of. Remember from whom you learned
them; remember that from early childhood you have been
familiar with the sacred writings which have power to make
you wise and lead you to salvation through faith in Christ
Jesus.

2 Timothy 3: 14–15

T ake your share of hardship, like a good soldier of Christ
Jesus. A soldier on active service will not let himself be
involved in civilian affairs; he must be wholly at his com-
manding officer's disposal. Again, no athlete can win a prize
unless he has kept the rules. The farmer who gives his labour
has first claim on the crop. Reflect on what I say, for the
Lord will help you to full understanding.

2 Timothy 2: 3–7

But let us, who are of the day, be sober, putting on the breastplate of faith and love; and for an helmet, the hope of salvation.

For God hath not appointed us to wrath, but to obtain salvation by our Lord Jesus Christ,

Who died for us, that, whether we wake or sleep, we should live together with him.

Wherefore comfort yourselves together, and edify one another.

1 Thessalonians 5: 8–11

BE NOT MOVED AWAY

If ye continue in the faith grounded and settled, and be not moved away from the hope of the gospel, which ye have heard, and which was preached to every creature which is under heaven; whereof I Paul am made a minister.

Colossians 1: 23

We, who belong to daylight, must keep sober, armed with faith and love for breastplate, and the hope of salvation for helmet. For God has not destined us to the terrors of judgement, but to the full attainment of salvation through our Lord Jesus Christ. He died for us so that we, awake or asleep, might live in company with him. Therefore hearten one another, fortify one another.

1 *Thessalonians* 5: 8–11

NEVER BE DISLODGED

Only you must continue in your faith, firm on your foundations, never to be dislodged from the hope offered in the gospel which you heard. This is the gospel which has been proclaimed in the whole creation under heaven; and I, Paul, have become its minister.

Colossians 1: 23

To the acknowledgement of the mystery of God, and of the Father, and of Christ;

In whom are hid all the treasures of wisdom and knowledge.

Colossians 2: 2–3

YOU WHICH BELIEVE

Wherefore also it is contained in the scripture, Behold, I lay in Sion a chief corner stone, elect, precious: and he that believeth on him shall not be confounded.

Unto you therefore which believe he is precious: but unto them which be disobedient, the stone which the builders disallowed, the same is made the head of the corner,

And a stone of stumbling, and a rock of offence, even to them which stumble at the word, being disobedient: whereunto also they were appointed.

1 *Peter* 2: 6–8

THE SECRET IS CHRIST

Grasp God's secret. That secret is Christ himself; in him lie hidden all God's treasures of wisdom and knowledge.

Colossians 2: 2–3

YOU WHO HAVE FAITH

For it stands written:
   "I lay in Zion a choice corner-stone of great worth.
   The man who has faith in it will not be put to shame."
The great worth of which it speaks is for you who have faith. For those who have no faith, the stone which the builders rejected has become not only the corner-stone, but also "a stone to trip over, a rock to stumble against". They stumble when they disbelieve the Word. Such was their appointed lot!

1 *Peter* 2: 6–8

TRIED WITH FIRE

That the trial of your faith, being much more precious than of gold that perisheth, though it be tried with fire, might be found unto praise and honour and glory at the appearing of Jesus Christ.

I Peter I: 7

THE MILK OF THE WORD

Wherefore laying aside all malice, and all guile, and hypocrisies, and envies, and all evil speakings,

As newborn babes, desire the sincere milk of the word, that ye may grow thereby:

If so be ye have tasted that the Lord is gracious.

I Peter 2: 1–3

29TH DAY

STOOD THE TEST

Even gold passes through the assayer's fire, and more precious than perishable gold is faith which has stood the test. These trials come so that your faith may prove itself worthy of all praise, glory, and honour when Jesus Christ is revealed.

1 *Peter* 1: 7

THRIVE UPON IT

Then away with all malice and deceit, away with all pretence and jealousy and recrimination of every kind! Like the new-born infants you are, you must crave for pure milk (spiritual milk, I mean), so that you may thrive upon it to your souls' health. Surely you have tasted that the Lord is good.

1 *Peter* 2: 1–3

Be sober, be vigilant; because your adversary the devil, as a roaring lion, walketh about, seeking whom he may devour:

Whom resist stedfast in the faith, knowing that the same afflictions are accomplished in your brethren that are in the world.

But the God of all grace, who hath called us unto his eternal glory by Christ Jesus, after that ye have suffered a while, make you perfect, stablish, strengthen, settle you.

1 Peter 5: 8–10

LONGSUFFERING WITH YOU

But, beloved, be not ignorant of this one thing, that one day is with the Lord as a thousand years, and a thousand years as one day.

The Lord is not slack concerning his promise, as some men count slackness; but is longsuffering to us-ward, not willing that any should perish, but that all should come to repentance.

2 Peter 3: 8–9

30TH DAY

Awake! be on the alert! Your enemy the devil, like a roaring lion, prowls round looking for someone to devour. Stand up to him, firm in faith, and remember that your brother Christians are going through the same kinds of suffering while they are in the world. And the God of all grace, who called you into his eternal glory in Christ, will himself, after your brief suffering, restore, establish, and strengthen you on a firm foundation.

1 Peter 5: 8–10

VERY PATIENT WITH YOU

And here is one point, my friends, which you must not lose sight of: with the Lord one day is like a thousand years and a thousand years like one day. It is not that the Lord is slow in fulfilling his promise, as some suppose, but that he is very patient with you, because it is not his will for any to be lost, but for all to come to repentance.

2 Peter 3: 8–9

This then is the message which we have heard of him, and declare unto you, that God is light, and in him is no darkness at all.

If we say that we have fellowship with him, and walk in darkness, we lie, and do not the truth:

But if we walk in the light, as he is in the light, we have fellowship one with another, and the blood of Jesus Christ his Son cleanseth us from all sin.

1 John 1: 5-7

HE ABIDETH FOR EVER

Love not the world, neither the things that are in the world. If any man love the world, the love of the Father is not in him.

For all that is in the world, the lust of the flesh, and the lust of the eyes, and the pride of life, is not of the Father, but is of the world.

And the world passeth away, and the lust thereof: but he that doeth the will of God abideth for ever.

1 John 2: 15-17

31ST DAY

Here is the message we heard from him and pass on to you: that God is light, and in him there is no darkness at all. If we claim to be sharing in his life while we walk in the dark, our words and our lives are a lie; but if we walk in the light as he himself is in the light, then we share together a common life, and we are being cleansed from every sin by the blood of Jesus his Son.

1 John 1: 5–7

HE STANDS FOR EVERMORE

Do not set your hearts on the godless world or anything in it. Anyone who loves the world is a stranger to the Father's love. Everything the world affords, all that panders to the appetites, or entices the eyes, all the glamour of its life, springs not from the Father but from the godless world. And that world is passing away with all its allurements, but he who does God's will stands for evermore.

1 John 2: 15–17

31ST DAY